# Down by the River

Annette Smith
Photographs by Lindsay Edwards
Illustrations by Richard Hoit

## Contents

The Ducks 2

The Leaves 6

The Ants 8

The Spider 10

Going Home 12

Glossary 16

## The Ducks

Today, Dad and I
went for a big walk.

We went down
to the river
to look at the **ducks**.

Some little ducks

ran away.

They ran down the hill

and into the water.

A big duck

came up to me.

## The Leaves

I played in some **leaves** by a tree.

I liked the yellow leaves.

Dad liked the red leaves.

## The Ants

We looked at some ants
in the grass.

The ants ran
into a little hole
in a log.

# The Spider

Dad and I looked

at a big spider

on a tree.

The big spider looked

at Dad and me.

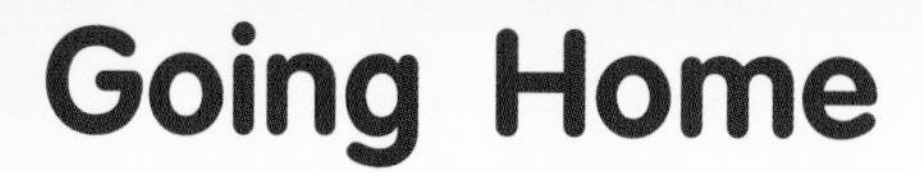

# Going Home

I ran down the path.

Dad ran after me.

Dad and I went home.

We had fun
down by the river.

# Glossary

**ducks**

**leaves**